Vitamins for the Spirit

A Collection of Insights to Enrich Your Every Day

Bob Danzig

Danzig Insight Services, Inc.

Vitamins for the Spirit

Published by Danzig Insight Services, Inc.
www.bobdanzig.com

ISBN: 978-0-9855129-4-1

Printed & Distributed by Lightning Source, Inc.
www.lightningsource.com

Illustration Credits On Page 70.

Vitamins for the Spirit

A Collection of Insights to Enrich Your Every Day

Bob Danzig

Gratitude

With great gratitude for the privilege of guiding Mary Elizabeth, Marsha Therese, Darcy Lynn, Steven Robert and Mathew Brady towards the unique "Vitamins for the Spirit" they are.

Acknowledgment

To all who provided me a favorite combination of words that can serve to inspire and the lovely, rare-in-the-universe pen and ink sketches of the gifted Hearst Newspapers artists, who shared their abundant creativity. Thank you!

Foreword

Preparing for a visit to my daughter, Darcy, in Dayton, Ohio – I had purchased a new personal organizer as a gift for her. While waiting for the accommodating sales lady to organize the organizer, my eyes set on a display rack of cards with motivational quotes. Knowing that Darcy enjoyed motivational quotes, I purchased several.

When I presented them to her, I noticed that they were simply quotes with no unifying theme. Darcy thanked me and asked, "What unifying quotes would you suggest if such cards were produced by you?"

My answer, after a moment's reflection, was to call them: "Vitamins for the Spirit." Darcy responded that this was a big idea and I should go home and trademark it. I did.

When the trademark validation arrived, I decided to collect vitamins from mainly strangers who crossed my path over a 2-week period.

Precisely 64 people came my way in 14 days. I asked that each send a favorite motivational thought by email or fax. Every single person did just that.

I then sent each quote to the art department of Hearst Newspapers and requested pen and ink sketches which reflected the artist's creative reaction to the motivating words. The result is this potpourri of lovely renderings – a source of inspiration to all who read and assimilate these pages.

Vitamins for the Spirit invites you to fill your day with inspiration.

VITAMINS
for the
SPIRIT

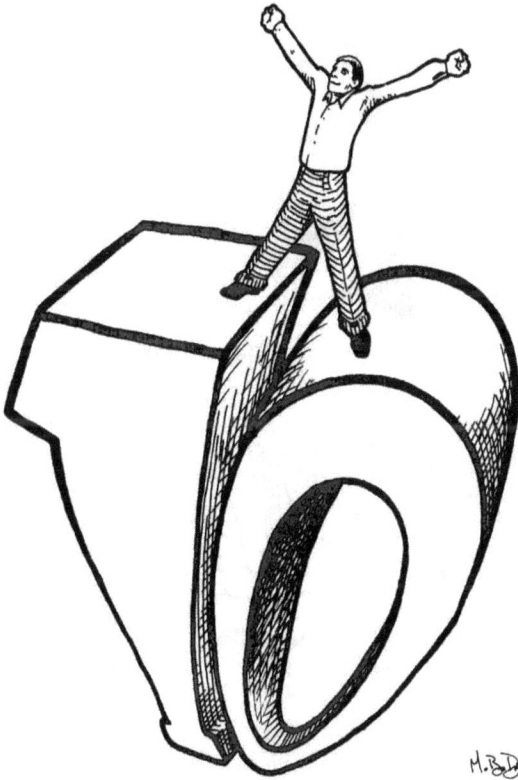

M.B. Dwozig 1996

The 10 most powerful two letter words:

IF IT IS TO BE

IT IS UP TO ME

ive words that stand
between you and your dream:

I don't feel like it

It is not **WHAT** you do for

a living that is most

important — but —

HOW WELL you do it that

makes the difference.

ope that is seen is not hope,
for who hopes for what he sees?
But, if we hope for what we do not see,
we wait for it with patience.

Never Complain.

Never Explain.

Embrace **THE THREADS OF LIFE**

that come your way.

They will weave together

to become the

tapestry of your life.

All glory comes
from daring to **BEGIN**.
Well done is
better than well **SAID**!

Vitamins for the Spirit

Many of life's
failures are persons who
did not realize how
CLOSE they were to **SUCCESS**
when they gave up.

The important thing in
this world is not so much
where we are — but — in what
direction we are moving.

M. B. Daniec

Do not wish to be

anything but what you are —

and try to be that

perfectly.

When you have done your

best-

You should wait for the result in

peace.

our **SPIRIT** *— your will to*

excel and endure.

These qualities are much more

important than the events that occur.

14

Four simple steps to accomplishment:

Plan purposefully

Prepare prayerfully

Proceed positively

Pursue persistently

We cannot direct the

winds-

but we can adjust the

sails.

Among your **wonders**

is the ability to:

$\mathscr{C}$HOOSE!

Enthusiasm is the

PROPELLING FORCE

for climbing

the ladder of success.

CHEER UP:

Birds have bills, too,

but they keep on

singing.

earn to pause...

Things worthwhile

can catch up to you.

Life is in session.
Are you present?

Everyone
is
someone.

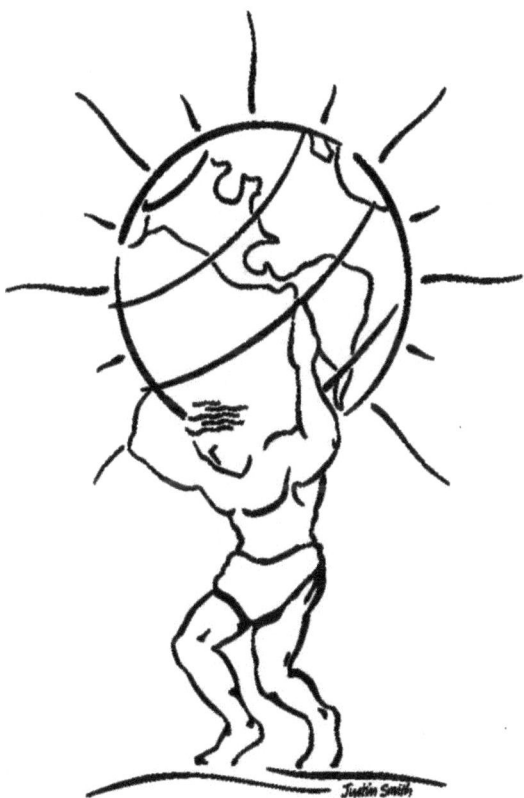

Justin Smith

Better to **fail** at
doing **SOMETHING**

than to
succeed
at doing **NOTHING.**

Mark Joseph Sharer

How silent the woods
would be if only
the best birds sang.

Give me the **SERENITY**
to accept what **CANNOT** be changed,

the **COURAGE** to
influence what **CAN** be changed,

and the **WISDOM** to know
one from the other.

Never let yesterday
use up
too much of today.

J.T.MENO

Things turn out best

for those who make the best

out of the way

things turn out.

27

Think *a good day!*

Plan *a good day!*

Put **good** *into the day!*

A bell is no *bell*
until you ring it.

A song is no *song*
until you sing it.

Love isn't *love* until
you give it away.

The single **BEST STEP** to advance
in your life work is to

Shine

where you
are potted.

PRESS ON

*Nothing in the world
can take the place of persistence.*

*Talent will not;
nothing is more common than
unsuccessful men with talent.*

*Genius will not;
unrewarded genius is almost a proverb.*

*Education — alone — will not;
the world is full of educated derelicts.*

*Persistence and determination
alone are omnipotent.*

Vitamins for the Spirit

CANDLE'S *but a simple*
thing, it starts with just
a bit of string.

Dipped with patient hand,
it gathers wax upon the strand,
until complete and snowy white
it gives at last a lovely light.

LIFE *seems so like that bit of string.*

Each time we do a simple thing,
yet day by day on life's strand,
we work with patient heart and hand.

It gathers joy, makes dark days bright
and **GIVES** *at last a lovely light.*

No life is so **HARD**
that one can't make it **EASIER**
by the way one **ACCEPTS** it.

QUINN-GRIMM

Life by the **mile** is a trial.

Life by the **yard** is hard.

But — life by the

inch is a cinch!

The will to win
is not nearly as important
as the will to

PREPARE to win.

Your mind is powerful
enough to do more than one thing
at one time, but you can only do
one thing **WELL** at one time.
Just do what you're doing
while you're doing it.

36

irst we form habits,

then they form us.

CONQUER *your bad habits,*

or they will eventually conquer you.

Do it!

Do it right!

Do it right now!

Vitamins for the Spirit

When your heart
is in your dreams — no request
is too extreme.

Vitamins for the Spirit

Adversity causes some
people to break and others
to break records.

Life is like a grindstone, it either grinds
you down or it polishes you up.

If better is possible,

good is not enough.

Edison was asked how he dealt
with the 12,000 failures he experienced
in inventing the light bulb.

He said he never failed —
he just learned 12,000 ways **NOT**
to invent the light bulb.

What losers call failure
winners call **FEEDBACK**!

ou drift toward the rocks;

you sail toward success.

So set sail, and if there

is no wind — row!

Be an action person.

Do not wait to get motivated

before you do something.

Do something and

then you will get motivated.

44

How to avoid criticism:

Say nothing

Do nothing

Be nothing

If you do not

stretch

your limits, you will

SET your limits.

Everything you need
is already inside you.
An acorn has everything
it needs to become an oak.

You alone, just you.
Only you can
SHARE
YOUR
ESSENCE.

A painter paints with his **HAND**.

An artist paints with his **MIND**.

But — a **master** paints

with his hand and his

mind through his **HEART**.

(RICHARD K. STODDARD)

inners are not

passionate because they are successful.

They are successful

because they are passionate.

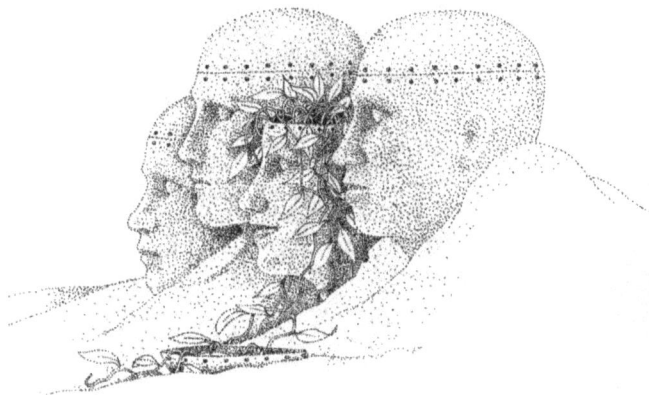

Your mind is
like a parachute —
it only works
when it is **OPEN**.

People are like ten-speed bikes — most of us have gears we never use.

MONITOR YOUR SELF-TALK.

The words "can't," "if," "impossible,"

"maybe" and "try" are in the dictionary.

But — they are NOT part of the

everyday vocabulary of WINNERS.

Shoot for the moon.

Even if you miss,

you will be among the stars.

Do not coast.
Nothing ever
coasts **UPHILL**.

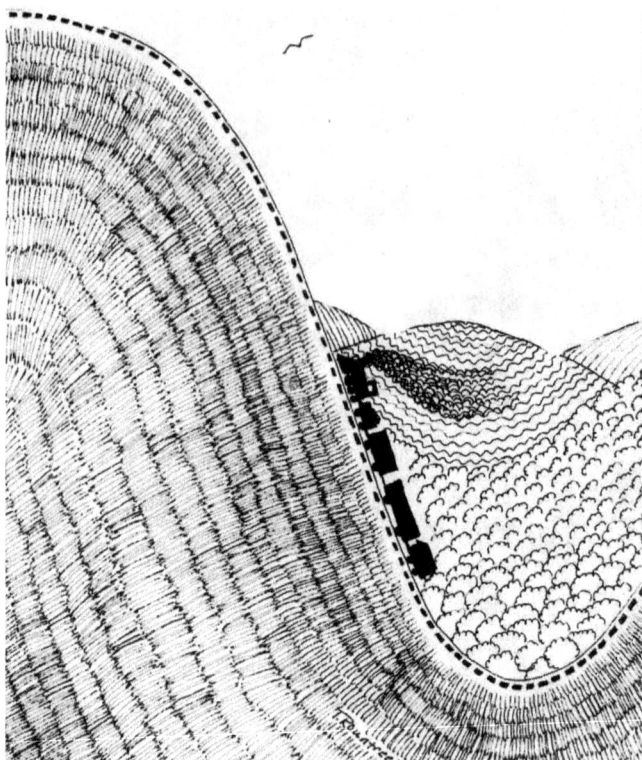

hether you think you **CAN** or
whether you think you **CAN'T** —
you are right in either case.

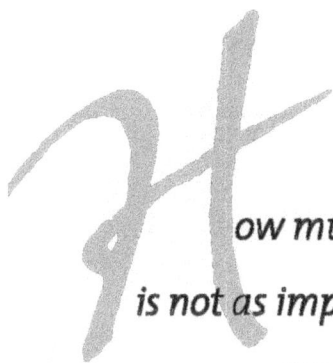

How much time you **PUT IN** is not as important as what you **PUT INTO** the time.

Your greatest gift in
conversations is to

*L*isten
Aggressively.

Act the way you want

to **BECOME** and you will

become the way you **ACT**.

You make a **living** by
what you GET.

You make a **life** by
what you GIVE.

5 keys to happiness:

Health

Love

Achievement

Expectation

Contrast

61

Vitamins for the Spirit

Ignite the leader within you. Polish up your:

Quality

Innovation

Inspiration

Perseverance

Passion & Enthusiasm

Character

Charisma & Energy

What a day
a
difference makes.

What you conceive in your

mind and believe

in your **heart** you

will achieve.

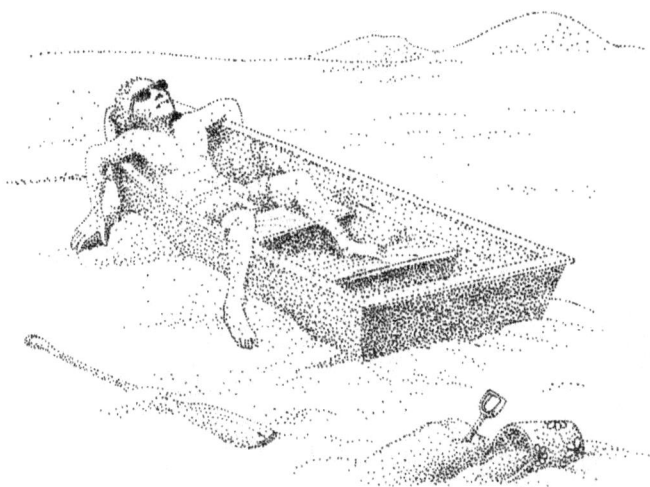

*f you do not know
where you are going you
might end up where
you are heading.*

A mistake is not failure — but feedback.

J.T. MENO

Winning does not lead to

passion; passion leads to

winning.

Love is invariably a two-way street —
a reciprocal phenomena
whereby the receiver also
gives and the giver also receives.

Everyone wants to be loved.
But — first we must make
ourselves lovable. We'll do this by
becoming a loving person.

69

The Illustrators

A special thanks to all of the wonderful
artists who donated their talents.

Vitamins for the Spirit

Artist		Affiliation
Mathew B. Danzig	3	Wet Squirrel, Ltd.
Mathew B. Danzig	4	Wet Squirrel, Ltd.
Sally Quinn-Grimm	5	*Midland Daily News*
Dan de la Torre	6	*San Francisco Examiner*
Mathew B. Danzig	7	*Wet Squirrel, Ltd.*
Jill Feuk	8	*Houston Chronicle*
Mathew B. Danzig	9	*Wet Squirrel, Ltd.*
Doug Moore	10	*Albany Times Union*
Patrick Zeller	11	*San Antonio Express-News*
Mathew B. Danzig	12	*Wet Squirrel, Ltd.*
John T. Valles	13	*Midland Reporter Telegram*
Holly Maltby	14	*Midland Daily News*
Joe Shoulak	15	*San Francisco Examiner*
Beena Mayekar	16	*Houston Chronicle*
Jeff Scheer	18	*Albany Times Union*
Mathew B. Danzig	19	*Wet Squirrel, Ltd.*
John T. Valles	20	*Midland Reporter Telegram*
Sally Quinn-Grimm	21	*Midland Daily News*
Dan de la Torre	22	*San Francisco Examiner*
Justin Smith	23	*Houston Chronicle*
Mark Joseph Share	24	*Albany Times Union*

Artist		Affiliation
Patrick Zeller	25	*San Antonio Express-News*
Steve Greenberg	26	*Seattle Post-Intelligencer*
Judith Tate Meno	27	*Midland Daily News*
Dan de la Torre	28	*San Francisco Examiner*
Inho Kim	29	*Houston Chronicle*
Doug Moore	31	*Albany Times Union*
John Camejo	32	*San Antonio Express-News*
Ben Garrison	33	*Seattle Post-Intelligencer*
Sally Quinn-Grimm	34	*Midland Daily News*
Joe Shoulak	35	*San Francisco Examiner*
Beena Mayekar	36	*Houston Chronicle*
Rex Babin	37	*Albany Times Union*
Felipe Soto	38	*San Antonio Express-News*
John T. Valles	39	*Midland Reporter Telegram*
Mathew B. Danzig	40	Wet Squirrel, Ltd.
Staff Artist	41	Hearst Newspapers
Jill Feuk	42	*Houston Chronicle*
Greg Montgomery	43	*Albany Times Union*
John Camejo	44	*San Antonio Express-News*
Kim Carney	45	*Seattle Post-Intelligencer*
Holly Maltby	46	*Midland Daily News*

Artist		Affiliation
Joe Shoulak	47	*San Francisco Examiner*
Justin Smith	49	*Houston Chronicle*
Richard K. Stoddard	50	*Albany Times Union*
Felipe Soto	51	*San Antonio Express-News*
Cliff Vancura	52	*Seattle Post-Intelligencer*
Sally Quinn-Grimm	53	*Midland Daily News*
Gene McDavid	54	*Houston Chronicle*
Terry Rountree	55	*Houston Chronicle*
Doug Moore	56	*Albany Times Union*
James Hendricks	59	*San Antonio Express-News*
Duane Hoffman	60	*Seattle Post-Intelligencer*
Rebecca Agler	61	*Midland Daily News*
Mathew B. Danzig.	62	Wet Squirrel, Ltd.
Terry Rountree	63	*Houston Chronicle*
Rex Babin	64	*Albany Times Union*
Felipe Soto	65	*San Antonio Express-News*
John T. Valles	66	*Midland Reporter Telegram*
Judith Tate Meno	67	*Midland Daily News*
Joe Shoulak	68	*San Francisco Examiner*
Inho Kim	69	*Houston Chronicle*
Richard K. Stoddard	70	*Albany Times Union*